MW01716714

A Palace in Time

A PJ Library Family Guide to SHABBAT

A Palace in Time

A holiday that comes every week? What a concept!

The idea of Shabbat — a sacred day of rest — is rooted in Judaism's most ancient sources: in the creation story that begins the biblical book of Genesis, in the account of the Jewish people's 40-year desert wandering after escaping slavery in Egypt, and even in the Ten Commandments themselves.

How profound it is that such an ancient idea is still so relevant today. Our world can get messy and overwhelming. Our lives can feel busy and sometimes stressful. Life can be competitive even for young children. And, of course, there's the nonstop barrage of technology. How do we just slow things down?

Shabbat is a regular gift to ourselves, a time to be together, celebrate, and nourish our souls. When the sun sets on Friday evening, no matter how our week has been — whatever its highs and lows — Shabbat is here. And since Shabbat comes every week, there's plenty of opportunity for trying out new things — new rituals and activities, new stories, songs, and conversations, new foods and faces.

As 20th-century philosopher and activist Rabbi Abraham Joshua Heschel wrote in his book *The Sabbath*, "The seventh day is a palace in time which we build." This guide can support your family as you're building.

Shabbat shalom! A peaceful Sabbath!

There is a day
when the road neither
comes nor goes, and the way
is not a way but a place.

— Wendell Berry (20th-century American writer)

What's in This Guide?

This guide offers ways for families to celebrate Shabbat at home. Because each family is unique, the guide is designed so you can choose those parts that meet the needs and interests of your family. Each section of the guide offers a different "pillar" of Shabbat, with explanations, sources, and tips for celebrating as a family.

Three Pillars of Shabbat

Introducing Shabbat through three core concepts

Step-by-Step Rituals

Bringing Shabbat traditions into your home

Hands-On Activities and Recipes

Over 20 different family projects to add fun and meaning to your Shabbat experience

Sounds of Shabbat

A playlist of special Shabbat songs through the ages, plus additional playlists of Shabbat blessings and table songs

Shabbat in Its Diversity

A global look at how Shabbat is prepared and practiced in the Jewish world

Conversation Starters

Questions, stories, and quotes to spark family discussions, including a game of Talking Cards

For Parents

Reflections about key Shabbat themes

A Shabbat Table Companion

A convenient handout with Shabbat blessings and songs

You don't need to read the whole guide in order to start experimenting. Shabbat comes every week, so pick any section and start there. The following week you can pick a different section.

For more resources, including a downloadable copy of the Shabbat Table Companion, visit pjlibrary.org/shabbat.

Contents

To help you share this guide with your children, we've put a symbol next to pages that are especially kid-friendly. Throughout the guide, Hebrew words will appear in italics — except the word "Shabbat"!

Shabbat is ... 6

REST

Rest (*Menucha*): the First Pillar 8

The Creation Story 11

What's "Rest," and How Do We Prepare for It? 17

Getting Ready for Shabbat 18

For Parents 25

A Peek Inside: How Different Families Prepare for Shabbat 26

ABUNDANCE

Abundance (*Shefa*): the Second Pillar 28

Lighting Shabbat Candles 30

Welcoming Shabbat (*Kabbalat Shabbat*) 32

Blessing the Children 34

Special Shabbat Guests: Angels and a Queen 36

Kiddush (Blessing Over Wine or Grape Juice) 38

Washing Hands and Eating Challah 42

The Double Portion of Manna (Exodus, chapter 16) 46

The Shabbat Meal Around the World 48

The Traditional Rhythm of Shabbat 49

PRESENCE

Presence (*Panim*): the Third Pillar 50

The Song of Songs 53

13 Ways for Families to Connect on Shabbat 57

Shabbat Conversations 58

Shabbat Songs 59

Shabbat Stories 60

Shabbat Search-and-Find 62

Broadening the Circle: Shabbat in Community 64

For Parents 65

HAVDALAH

Havdalah (Separation) 66

Epilogue 70

Talking Cards 71

A set of removable cards for Jewish reflection and discussion

Shabbat Table Companion

Included with this guide is a separate compendium of blessings and songs for use at your Shabbat table

Shabbat is...

A World-Shaping Idea

The idea of Shabbat changed history. Until that point, religious and political authorities commanded people only to work. Then in the Ten Commandments (specifically, the fourth one), people — even animals — are commanded to rest.

Shabbat shifts the way we experience time.

As the modern Jewish thinker Abraham Joshua Heschel writes in *The Sabbath,*

> What was the first holy object in the history of the world? A mountain? An altar? ... In the Book of Genesis, at the end of the story of creation, the word *qadosh* [holy] appears and is applied to time: "And God blessed the seventh day and made it holy."
>
> This is a radical departure from accustomed religious thinking. The mythical mind would expect that, after heaven and earth have been established, God would create a holy place whereupon a sanctuary is to be established. Yet it seems as if, to the Bible, it is holiness in time — the Sabbath — which comes first.
>
> Judaism is a religion of time ... ***The Sabbaths are our great cathedrals*** ... Six days a week we wrestle with the world, wringing profit from the earth ... On the Sabbath we are called upon to share in what is eternal in time, to turn from the world of creation to the creation of the world.

How can Shabbat shape your experience of time?

A Family-Shaping Idea

One of the powers of a holiday that comes every week is its unique ability to imprint important values on our children. Here are some of the traditional Jewish values embedded in the practice of Shabbat:

Peace (*Shalom* שָׁלוֹם)

Once a week, Shabbat can help create a different tone and rhythm in the home. When kids sense this shift, a certain serenity setting in, they often embrace it. This value is so intrinsic to Shabbat that the traditional Hebrew greeting we say before and on Shabbat is "*Shabbat shalom*" שַׁבַּת שָׁלוֹם (have a peaceful Sabbath).

Shalom bayit שָׁלוֹם בַּיִת ***(treating everyone in the family nicely, literally "peace in the home") is a value to aspire to all week long but especially on Shabbat.***

Joy (*Simcha* שִׂמְחָה)

Shabbat teaches us that life is worth celebrating on a very regular basis. (Kids often know this intuitively.) On Shabbat, we take joy in simple things: family, friends, food, song, stories. Just follow your kids' lead into Shabbat joy.

There's even a special term for Shabbat joy: **oneg Shabbat** **עוֹנֶג שַׁבָּת.**

Awe/Gratitude

(*Hakarat hatov* הַכָּרַת הַטּוֹב)

Shabbat is a time for stepping back and appreciating the big and little wonders of the world: a gorgeous sunset, a warm challah (braided bread), and more. On Shabbat we can literally count our blessings, and our kids will open themselves to gratitude.

Family, Friendship, and Community

(*Mishpacha*, *Chaverut*, and *Kehilla* מִשְׁפָּחָה, חֲבֵרוּת, וְקְהִלָּה)

All of our most basic social frameworks need to be nurtured. Shabbat creates space for exactly that: quality time for family, relaxed meals with friends and newcomers, and connections (with shared joys and sorrows) within a prayer or learning community.

When we invite people to our homes for Shabbat (in Hebrew, hachnasat orchim הַכְנָסַת אוֹרְחִים or "welcoming guests"), our children learn to be friendly, curious, and gracious.

Justice (*Tzedek* צֶדֶק)

Shabbat is a great leveler. It doesn't matter if you're a worker or a boss, a local or a stranger, a grownup or a child — we all get to rest. This celebration of justice takes a very concrete form in many homes. Right before Shabbat, everyone empties their pockets of coins to place in the family *tzedakah* box (a box for collecting charitable contributions), so even as we take a break from worldly concerns, we express our commitment to a decent, more just society.

SOUNDS OF SHABBAT

Ma Yafeh Hayom

מַה יָּפֶה הַיּוֹם

Such a beautiful day/

A peaceful Sabbath

A 20th-century American Jewish song

Rest

מְנוּחָה

(*menucha,* pronounced meh-noo-CHAH)

The first pillar of Shabbat is rest. The Hebrew word *Shabbat* שַׁבָּת means “to cease”— especially, to stop working. Another Hebrew word for rest is *menucha* מְנוּחָה.

Pretend you’re floating at sea. (*Menucha* shares a Hebrew root with the name *Noah* נֹחַ, the original floater-at-sea.) No chores, no Internet, no place to rush off to. Just the feeling of warm sunlight on your face.

That’s rest. Your body needs to rest, and so does your soul. When the Torah (the first five books of the Bible) says “God worked for six days creating the world and then rested,” it immediately adds “*vayinafash*” וַיִּנָּפַשׁ, “and God ‘resouled.’”

Our lives are busy. By the end of the week, we’re tired out. How do we rest? Each family needs to answer that question for themselves, but there are many possibilities offered by the 3,000-year-old Jewish mindfulness practice called Shabbat.

SOUNDS OF SHABBAT

Shir Ha'emek

שִׁיר הָעֵמֶק

(Song of the Valley)

Rest comes for the weary/
Relaxation for the worker
Sleep, dear valley/Land of
glorious beauty

A Hebrew song sung by secular pioneers who founded Israel's first kibbutzim *(collective farms) in the 1920s*

After the six days of creation, what did the universe still lack? Menucha. Came the Sabbath, came menucha, and the universe was complete.

— Midrash (rabbinic interpretation) on Genesis 2:2

How do you rest?

"Six days you will labor and do all your work" (Exodus 20:9). But is it possible for us to do all our work in six days? Rather, we should rest as though all our work were finished.

— *Mechilta Yitro 7*

Menucha points us toward the **intention** we bring to Shabbat — how we anticipate the day of rest and how we prepare for it.

1 One way to think about Shabbat is as the "pause that refreshes" when you and your family recharge your batteries for the week to come. You bring more energy to your weekdays because you've experienced *menucha* on Shabbat.

But another way to think about Shabbat is expressed in the Zohar, a classic work of Jewish mystical thought: "The Sabbath is not for the sake of the weekdays; the weekdays are for the sake of Sabbath." 2

3 In other words, **Shabbat is not the break in the action. It's the main event.**

We see this second approach in how days of the week are referred to in Hebrew. Days don't have unique names; there are no Tuesdays or Thursdays. In Hebrew, there's simply *Yom Rishon* יוֹם רִאשׁוֹן ("first day"), *Yom Sheni* יוֹם שֵׁנִי ("second day"), all the way until the sun sets at the close of the sixth day (Friday) — and then we welcome Shabbat.

So the whole week we're counting our way toward Shabbat. By this second approach, Shabbat is a much-anticipated and much-prepared-for event.

This second approach mirrors the biblical creation story in Genesis, in which Shabbat is the grand finale. So let's revisit that story and then explore ways in which families might get ready for — and excited about — Shabbat.

What do you look forward to about Shabbat?

SOUNDS OF SHABBAT

Bulbes

באלבעס (Potatoes)

Sunday, potatoes, Monday, potatoes,
Tuesday and Wednesday, potatoes,
Thursday and Friday, potatoes/But on
Shabbat — potato soup!

A Yiddish song sung in the shtetls (small villages) of eastern and central Europe

The Creation Story

In the beginning

בְּרֵאשִׁית ...

... the world was still unformed.

On the first day,

God said , "Let there be light!" And there was light.

On the second day,

God said, “Let’s separate waters
above from waters below!”
And there was sky.

On the third day,

God said, “Let the earth sprout plants!”
And there were trees, fruits, and
every kind of vegetation.

On the fourth day,

God said, "Let lights shine
down on Earth!"
And there was a sun, a moon,
and many stars.

On the fifth day,

God said, "Let creatures swim through
the sea and fly through the sky!"
And there were fish and birds.

On the *sixth* day,

God said, "Let animals fill the earth!"
And there were creeping things and
wild beasts of every imaginable kind.

Then God took a deep breath
and said, "Now let's make a being
in the image of God!"
and God formed human beings.

With this, the work of making a world —
sky, earth, and sea, all full of creatures — was done.

On the seventh day, God rested

and blessed the seventh day and called it holy.

"I like to rest on Shabbat. But did <u>God</u> really need to rest on Shabbat?"

God rested to show us that <u>our</u> creations (like God's) become meaningful only when we stop creating them and think about why we're bothering to create them at all.

— The Vilna Gaon (18th-century Lithuanian scholar)

What do <u>you</u> think the "image of God" means? ?

"The first Shabbat": a modern *midrash*
(creative interpretation of biblical text) in which all the works of creation come forward to help make the first Shabbat

SOUNDS OF SHABBAT

Shabbat Shalom

שַׁבָּת שָׁלוֹם

(Sabbath Peace)

from *The Creation: A Musical in Seven Days*

SUN: I'll humbly sink into the west
To usher in the day of rest

Shabbat begins when the sun sets on Friday evening and ends when three stars appear in the sky on Saturday night. (It's 25 hours long!)

STARS: And we three stars will then appear
To tell the world a new week is here

GRAPEVINE: We'll give the fruit of the vine
To show that life is sweet as wine

It's customary on Shabbat to say three blessings – over Shabbat lights, over wine or grape juice, and over bread.

WHEAT: And out of wheat a special bread
To show that the earth will keep us well-fed

LIGHT: Recalling what now seems long ago
We'd like to give this day a glow

BIRDS: And we'll be sure to add our share
Of gentle music in the air

ANGELS: We angels, last but far from least
We welcome you, and offer you the gift of peace

Some families sing a Friday-night song ("Shalom Aleichem," "Peace Be Upon You"), which describes angels of peace visiting our homes on Shabbat.

Shabbat Shalom
Shalom, Shabbat!

What's "Rest," and How Do We Prepare for It?

The ancient rabbis asserted that to understand rest (*menucha* מְנוּחָה), one must first understand work (*melacha* מְלָאכָה). They defined work in a very precise way — namely, all the tasks required for the Jewish people, as they wandered in the desert after escaping slavery in Egypt, to build a portable sanctuary (*mishkan* מִשְׁכָּן) as a "dwelling place for God." These tasks included the following:

- **Agricultural work** like planting and harvesting (for breads, dyes, and other items involved in sanctuary rites)
- **Food preparation** like kneading and baking (for meals and offerings)
- **Crafts** like weaving and sewing (for ornamental curtains and other ritual items)
- **Construction work** like building and demolishing
- **Other tasks related to the sanctuary project** like writing, buying and selling, riding, carrying, or making a fire

Families who observe Shabbat according to traditional Jewish law follow guidelines derived from this rabbinic construct. The transition from weekday to Shabbat becomes very dramatic: All food is cooked in advance, cars are parked for the duration of Shabbat, wallets get put away, computers and phones are turned off. The lead-up to Shabbat can be hectic, but then the world suddenly grows quiet.

Today, many families celebrate Shabbat in a less traditional way. Rest is a fluid concept. Heschel describes Shabbat as "the silence of abstaining from noisy acts," and nowadays, each family explores for itself which noisy acts will get toned down on Shabbat.

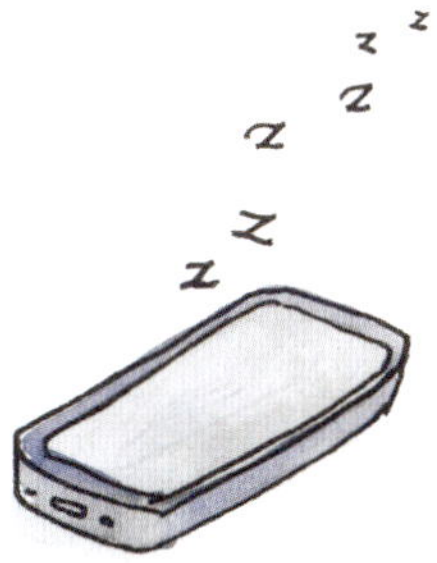

One huge challenge is **screen time**. Some families choose to unplug — for a meal, for a few hours, or for all or much of Shabbat. Unplugging is a new form of silence (one the ancient rabbis couldn't anticipate!) that creates a different atmosphere and can support family togetherness.

Because the concept of rest is more fluid, preparations for Shabbat grow all the more important in defining one's Shabbat experience and distinguishing Shabbat from other days of the week. These preparations can often become as special as Shabbat itself — especially when kids participate in the preparation.

In the following pages, you'll find tips on preparing for Shabbat so "when Shabbat comes, *menucha* comes."

Getting Ready for Shabbat

PLAN AHEAD

Make a Menu

A festive meal on Friday night makes Shabbat feel special. Some families lean into traditional family recipes. See some of PJ Library's favorite recipes at **pjlibrary.org/shabbat**.

Shopping for the right ingredients can be part of Shabbat preparation. (If you happen to be in Jerusalem, try shopping at the Machane Yehuda open-air market, itself a sumptuous feast of sights, smells, and tastes.)

If you don't have time to cook and Friday night is pizza-takeout night, you can still prep some special toppings or buy a special dessert to top off the meal.

Shabbat is when we enjoy delicacies
Cooked geese, quail, and fish

— 14th century Shabbat song

Invite Guests

Shabbat is an especially sweet time for relaxing with friends. It's also an opportunity to get to know families and individuals you don't know as well. *Hachnasat orchim* הַכְנָסַת אוֹרְחִים (welcoming guests) is a prime Jewish value, and Shabbat can bring that value home for everyone. Invite your guests far enough in advance so your kids can look forward to hosting and help you prepare.

Prepare a Shabbat Resting Kit

What things help your family relax together? Gather them up before Shabbat in your own Shabbat resting kit.

Supplies: large basket, tote bag, or box; favorite activities (such as books, toys, and games)

Directions: Pack your basket, bag, or box with items you and your family can enjoy together, like books (PJ Library and others), cards and board games, toys, yummy snacks, and more.

If the weather is nice, grab a picnic blanket and take your kit to the yard or a park. You can change what's in your kit from Shabbat to Shabbat, but consider keeping some of your favorites as regulars. If you choose, decorate your basket, bag, or box with colorful pictures that show what Shabbat means to your family.

Make a Shabbat Cover

Many families are familiar with the custom of placing a cover over challah (the braided Shabbat bread). Here's an idea for a multipurpose Shabbat cover.

TO MAKE YOUR COVER:

Take a piece of fabric (new or recycled). With paints or fabric markers, decorate the cloth with pictures of your family members, Shabbat ritual items, things you like to do on Shabbat, or scenes from the biblical creation story. Or write the word *Shabbat* (in Hebrew, שַׁבָּת) on your cover and add your own lovely pattern around it.

WHAT CAN YOU DO WITH YOUR COVER? Think out of the box!

- **Cover that surprise Shabbat dessert** (if it's not too gooey) so it's ready for the big reveal.
- **Cover a stuffie** when it takes a nap on Shabbat. (We can all use a Shabbat nap.)
- **Cover a cell phone or tablet** to welcome uninterrupted family time, especially during a Shabbat meal.
- **Cover your tzedakah box** and unveil it just before Shabbat so your family can add coins to it.
- **Cover a coffee table** to make it look festive for Shabbat.
- **Cover your face** and play Shabbat peekaboo with a baby sibling.
- **Cover the center of your dining room table** and place a vase of flowers on it.
- **Cover the PJ Library book** you've chosen to read on Shabbat — and pull off the Shabbat cover when it's time to read together.

Of course, you can also use it to cover your challah.

MAKE RITUALS SPECIAL

Bake Your Own Challah

Nothing says "Shabbat" more than home-baked challah. Your kids can be your helpers.

INGREDIENTS

To make two challah loaves, you'll need:
1½ tbsp yeast
2½ cups warm water
1 tsp plus ½ cup sugar
½ cup vegetable oil
1 tbsp salt
8 cups flour
1 cup raisins (optional)

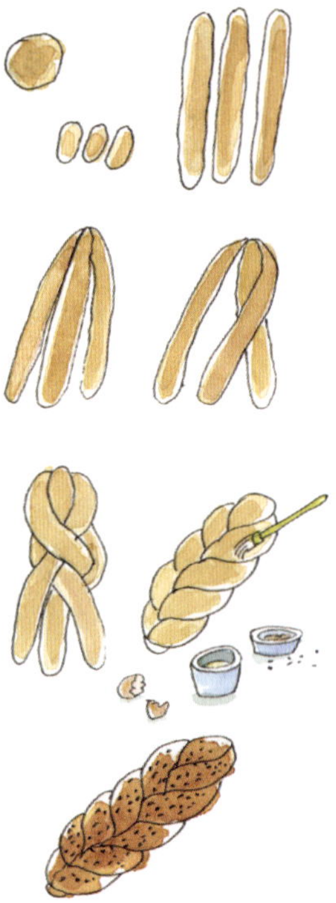

DIRECTIONS

Dissolve the yeast in the water with 1 teaspoon of sugar. Whisk the mixture together, then add the oil, salt, and remaining sugar. Add the flour gradually, mixing well and then working it in with your hands. Take turns kneading as a family for about 10-15 minutes, until the dough is smooth and elastic. Work in the raisins (optional). Cover the bowl with a towel and leave it in the refrigerator overnight. The next morning, let the dough warm to room temperature, then punch it down and separate into two portions.

TO BRAID: Separate the dough into three equal pieces. Roll each one into a long strand. Connect the three strands at the top. Put the right strand over the center one. Then weave the left strand over the new center piece. Keep going!

Bake at 350° for 20-25 minutes or until golden brown.

When you braid challah using three strands, it forms 12 "bumps" where braids have crisscrossed; this is symbolic of the 12 tribes of ancient Israel.

Customize Your Challah

Feeling adventurous? Try these challah add-ins.

SEEDS: After braiding the loaves and brushing them with egg wash, sprinkle different seeds (sesame, poppy, sunflower, pumpkin) on different strands of your challah.

SPICES: Mix 1 tablespoon of ground ginger, ½ teaspoon of ground cloves, and a ½ teaspoon of nutmeg into the challah dough.

CHOCOLATE: Add 1 cup of chocolate chips to the dough before you start kneading.

RAINBOW: After braiding the loaves and brushing them with egg wash, cover them liberally with rainbow sprinkles.

And then, of course, there are **shapes**. Traditional challah is always braided. But it's fun to go another step — take your braided challah and make it into a unique shape! Here are some popular ones: **sunflower, crown, star, fish, dove, pomegranate, candlestick, key,** and **Torah scroll.**

Since a different portion of the Torah is read every Shabbat, some families even try to shape their challah to illustrate something from the weekly Torah portion (when possible). Think **snake, tree, ark, rainbow** ... you get the idea. Good luck!

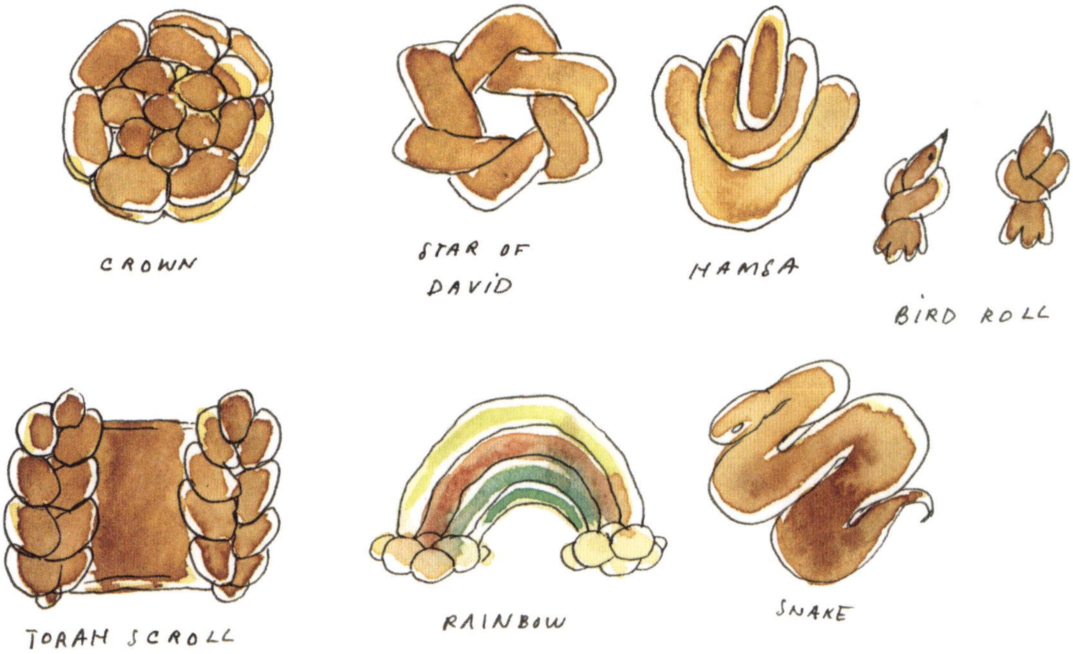

Make Candleholders

If your child joins you for Shabbat candle lighting, how fun for them to use these homemade candleholders!

SUPPLIES:

1 cup flour	Cookie cutters
½ cup salt	Candles
½ cup warm (not hot) water	Craft paint

DIRECTIONS: Mix flour and salt together in a medium-sized bowl, then add water and stir to combine. Knead the dough for about five minutes.

When the dough is fully kneaded, divide it into four balls, and place the balls on a parchment-lined baking sheet. Flatten the balls into circles, then use a cookie cutter to shape each one into a heart, Star of David, or whatever you like. Press a candle into the center of each shape, wiggle it, then remove it; you'll be left with a candle-shaped hole.

Bake the candleholders at 250° for three hours, or simply leave the candleholders out overnight to dry.

When candleholders are fully dried, paint them however you like. It is important to line the holders with foil before lighting. Shabbat shalom!

Make Grape Juice

Perhaps your kids have tried their hand at challah baking or even made a kiddush cup for the blessing over wine or grape juice. But have they ever tried this? (It's a messy sensory experience they won't soon forget ...)

SUPPLIES: Wash tub or large bowl, grapes

1. Wash child's feet thoroughly. **2.** Place grapes in the tub or bowl. **3.** Encourage your child to jump up and down (hold their hand so they don't slip) to mash the grapes. Or, if you prefer, just squish them with your hands. **4.** All ready for Shabbat — drink it if you dare!

Make a Shabbat Play Table

Kids can prepare for Shabbat by playing at their own miniature Shabbat table. Set up a small table (or inverted box) with Shabbat items. Balls of play dough can be shaped into candlesticks (place unlit candles in them) and challah. A small cup can be wrapped in tinfoil to be a kiddush cup. Don't forget the most important part: guests! Invite some stuffed animals and dolls to enjoy a festive Shabbat meal.

SET THE TONE AND THE TABLE

Listen to Music

What better way to get into the Shabbat spirit than with music! Put on a playlist while your family is cooking, baking, or setting the table. (See page 59 for PJ Library's custom Shabbat playlists.) And if the spirit moves you, dance!

Put Flowers on the Table

Let nature beautify your Shabbat table. Buy flowers or pick them from your garden. Time permitting, take a pre-Shabbat walk to find fun things in nature and bring some home to ornament your Shabbat table.

Or have your kids make their own "homegrown" flowers:

SUPPLIES: pen or pencil, colorful construction paper or card stock, scissors, glitter glue (optional), glue, green pipe cleaners

DIRECTIONS: Draw flower shapes on the paper of your choice and cut them out. Make them extra fancy with glitter glue if you wish. Use glue to attach a green pipe cleaner stem to the back of each one . When they're dry, place the flowers in a vase, put them on the table, and enjoy your lovely bouquet.

Make a DIY Tablecloth

A table can bring us together on Shabbat — and your kids can put their imprint on the table!

SUPPLIES: roll of butcher paper or white easel paper, scissors, tape, markers, crayons and/or colored pencils, stickers

DIRECTIONS: Cover the length of your table with the paper, then cut the piece(s) and tape to secure the "tablecloth" for Shabbat dinner. Use markers and more to draw Shabbat items (challah, candles, the food your family is cooking), portraits of your family (and guests!), or scenes of what you look forward to doing on Shabbat. Add stickers for an extra flourish.

If a tablecloth feels too ambitious, try making place mats instead.

Make Place Cards for Guests

Make your Shabbat guests feel especially welcome..

SUPPLIES: large index cards, craft supplies (crayons, markers, colored pencils, and/or stickers)

DIRECTIONS: Fold the index cards in half so they stand up like tents. If the index cards are lined, make sure the blank side is facing out. Write each guest's name on a card and decorate as you please. Place a card at each seat around the table.

SPECIAL CHALLENGE: Draw a picture on each card to represent a different day of the creation story. Can your guest guess which day it is?

FINAL STEPS

Get Dressed Up

Shabbat can feel more special when the family dresses up a bit. What would you like to wear? A special shirt? Special socks? Maybe even a crown so the Shabbat queen will feel at home. (You'll meet the Shabbat queen in the next section of this guide.)

Shake off your dust. Arise!
Put on your glorious garments, my people.
— Lecha Dodi, a traditional Shabbat prayer

Wish Someone "*Shabbat Shalom*"

Is there anyone you won't be seeing on Shabbat who would appreciate a phone call or video call? Call them and wish them "*Shabbat shalom!*"

Give Tzedakah

For some families, one of the last acts before entering Shabbat — when we try to rest our minds from the challenges of everyday life — is to donate a bit of money to causes that help fix the world (in Hebrew, *tikkun olam* תִיקוּן עוֹלָם). It's customary to empty one's pockets and wallets of coins or small bills and add them to your tzedakah box.

Use your PJ Library tzedakah box (or any other). Talk as a family where you want the money to go and why.

Turning On Shabbat

by Aliza Kline

Growing up, my home was pretty hectic: three kids, two working parents, a dog, a cat, and a turtle. On Fridays our house was especially bustling between laundry, grocery shopping, cooking, buying flowers, and setting a beautiful table for "company day."

When we were scrubbed clean, guests had been welcomed, and we were gathered around the table, it was time for my very special job. I concentrated hard, trying to time the flick of the light switch to the exact moment my mother struck the match to light the candles.

I imagined that I had the power to turn off the week and turn on Shabbat.

From so much running around to a moment of stillness — and sweetness. No need to eat my vegetables in order to get dessert. On Shabbat the rules were different, and, as I recall, chocolate milk flowed like a mighty river.

As a parent, I profoundly understand the need for this transition. We've added games to our Shabbat family dinner that help mark the shift: Our oldest will dress as a bride and dance into the dining room as we sing, "*Bo'i kallah*" ("Come on in, bride!"), embodying the kabbalistic (Jewish mystics') image of Shabbat. We make time on Shabbat for reading our favorite books, collecting leaves (season permitting), holding hands, and saying why we love each other. We lean into this time to be grateful, playful, and present.

There are too many moments I've missed as a parent, even when I was physically present (like being distracted while reading a bedtime story ... for the 100th time). Often we think of work and rest as two separate things entirely, and we do everything we can to avoid stopping. We want to cross off just one more task on the to-do list, and it's really hard to shut down.

On a recent road trip across Iceland, I found myself in the small city of Akureyri, where, strikingly, the stoplights have a red heart that lights up instead of a red circle. Shabbat is like a stop signal that tells us, "Wait! Slow down! Pay attention!" Without a pause, a break, or a rest, we risk missing moments with our children.

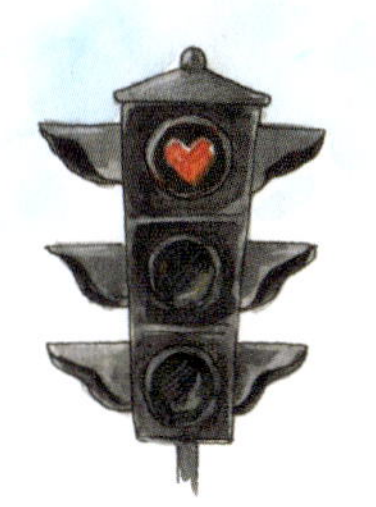

What's your heart-shaped stoplight? Jews are commanded to keep Shabbat, but we're not commanded to all do it in exactly the same way. What will your kids love and remember about Shabbat? What will delight and inspire them? How might they help turn on (or, on Saturday night, turn off) Shabbat?

Aliza Kline is the founding CEO of OneTable, which helps young adults across the US organize peer-led Shabbat dinners.

A PEEK INSIDE:

How Different Families Prepare for Shabbat

More than the Jewish people have kept Shabbat, Shabbat has kept the Jewish people.

— Ahad Ha'am (early 20th-century Hebrew author)

"We buy flowers every Friday afternoon for our Shabbat dinner table. It makes it feel like a holiday!"

"Whenever we have time, we bake challah rolls or a special dessert for Friday night. If we bake challah rolls, we even make a miniroll for our dog!"

"We're a traditional Yemenite family. We prepare our food in advance and put it on a *plata* (hot plate) to stay warm through Shabbat. We cover all the pots with dish towels to keep them extra warm."

"We live in London, and on Friday afternoon we gather for high tea. We eat cakes and biscuits and drink tea with milk to get into the Shabbat spirit."

"Our family custom is to write notes to each other sometime during the day and then open them at the Friday-night dinner table."

"We use the same floral tablecloth every Friday night. We put out nice dishes and silverware, and the kids like to fold napkins in a festive way."

"We have eight kids. Before Shabbat we lay out all the Shabbat clothes on our big bed in age order, and the kids take what's theirs to get dressed for Shabbat."

"On our kibbutz, the children's choir rehearses on Friday afternoon. When several hundred families gather in the dining hall for the Friday night meal, the kids sing. It's very special."

"The kids and I put on a playlist, and we work together to tidy up the playroom. We call out 'Shabbat is coming!' to keep ourselves on task."

שֶׁפַע

(*shefa*, pronounced SHEH-fah)

The second pillar of Shabbat is abundance — in Hebrew, *shefa*. So much of the week has been about getting things done. On Shabbat we can step back and take in the bigger picture —

The awesome wonders of nature. Loving family and friends. Things that give us hope and purpose. The many blessings in our lives.

Shabbat is a time to connect to something larger than ourselves: beauty, mystery, intimacy, joy, loving-kindness. (Some call these things God.)

In Jewish practice , this *shefa* (abundance) of blessings — and our gratitude for them — is expressed through three traditional Friday-night blessings: over the light of candles, over wine or grape juice, and over freshly baked challah (braided bread). It's not by chance that we begin Shabbat with these three blessings. In ancient Israel, abundance meant having enough oil for light, enough grapes for drink, and enough wheat for food. Today candles, wine, and challah help us celebrate our blessings and make the Shabbat meal festive.

Shabbat is a taste of the World to Come.

— *Babylonian Talmud*, Berachot 57A

Light a candle
Drink wine
Slowly the Sabbath descends
and in her hand
a flower,
and in her hand
the sinking sun.

— Zelda (20th-century Israeli poet)

SOUNDS OF SHABBAT

Mei'ein olam haba

מֵעֵין עוֹלָם הַבָּא

The day of rest is like the World to Come

A traditional Shabbat song

What are you grateful for this Shabbat?

Shefa points us toward the **tradition** of Shabbat, the powerful rituals that Jewish families have practiced generation after generation — and especially those rituals that help us welcome Shabbat.

When we begin a weekday, it's often a bit of a jolt — an alarm clock sounds, there's a mad scramble to leave the house. When we begin Shabbat, it's just the opposite. We take our cue from the sun. As the sun slowly slips beneath the horizon — a quiet, breath-stopping sight — we know Shabbat is coming in.

With the setting of the sun, a time when the world softens, a simple ritual act opens Shabbat: the lighting of Shabbat candles. It's a ritual that celebrates our sense of sight, bringing a warm light into our house.

In the Jewish calendar, each new day begins at sunset. That's because the creation story in Genesis says, "And there was evening, and there was morning, the first day."

Lighting Shabbat Candles

TIMING: It's traditional to light candles on Friday evening at sunset (according to Jewish law, 18 minutes before sunset). Many families choose to light candles whenever the family gathers for the Friday-night meal. In summertime with young kids, when sunset comes late, it's common to bring in Shabbat early.

NUMBER AND TYPE OF CANDLES: Some families light two candles. (Why two? See the explanation on page 45 for two challah breads.) Other families light one for each member of the family. Some Sephardi families light seven candles, one for each day of the week. Thick white candles are commonly used, but tea lights are also widespread (especially if you're lighting multiple candles).

WHO LIGHTS?: It's traditional for women to light and bless Shabbat candles, but the 12th-century scholar Maimonides writes, "The commandment to light candles applies to everyone."

THE RITUAL ITSELF: There's a simple choreography to the ritual. First, light the candles. Then cup your hands in front of you and slowly bring them toward you in a circular motion (as if you're scooping the light, drawing it toward you to illuminate all the blessings in your life). Perform this motion three times, then cover your eyes with your hands and say or sing the blessing over candles. Some add a silent prayer of healing or well wishes for someone. Then open your eyes and hug your family and friends, wishing them "*Shabbat shalom!*" — a peaceful Shabbat.

This beautiful choreography is easy for kids to imitate. TRY IT TOGETHER!

Candle-lighting blessing

בָּרוּךְ אַתָּה יְיָ אֱלֹהֵינוּ מֶלֶךְ הָעוֹלָם אֲשֶׁר קִדְּשָׁנוּ בְּמִצְוֹתָיו
וְצִוָּנוּ לְהַדְלִיק נֵר שֶׁל שַׁבָּת.

Baruch ata Adonai, Eloheinu melech ha'olam, asher kideshanu bemitzvotav vetzivanu lehadlik ner shel Shabbat.

Dear God, Creator of our world, thank You for giving us rules that make our lives special and for telling us to light the lights of Shabbat.

Only as an adult did I discover that I'm a descendant of Conversos, Jews who converted to Catholicism during the Spanish Inquisition of the 15th century and secretly practiced Judaism for generations. My grandmother lit candles on Friday evening. She'd wave her hands (without saying a blessing). No one knew why; it was just something we did. I always thought it was weird, until later I uncovered our Jewish roots. Now I've become Jewish, and Shabbat candle lighting is one of my favorite rituals.

— E.M., New Mexico

Do your Shabbat candlesticks have a family backstory?

(You might also think about a kiddush cup, a challah cover, or another Shabbat ceremonial item.) Share the story with your kids.

Welcoming Shabbat

(Kabbalat Shabbat)

After candle lighting, it's traditional for Jews to gather at synagogues or homes to welcome Shabbat with a special prayer service: *Kabbalat Shabbat* קַבָּלַת שַׁבָּת (welcoming the Sabbath).

The Kabbalat Shabbat service was created by the Jewish mystics of Tzfat in the Galil region of Israel 500 years ago. They would assemble at the base of the mountain (Tzfat sits at its top) and recite the poem *Yedid Nefesh* יְדִיד נֶפֶשׁ, in which God is called the Jewish people's "soul mate." Then they picked six biblical psalms — representing the six days of the week — to recite as they walked from the valley up the mountainside. When they reached the top, just in time to see the sun setting, they would sing *Lecha Dodi* לְכָה דוֹדִי ("Come, my friend!"), in which they imagined Shabbat coming closer and closer, like a bride walking down the aisle toward the *chuppah* חוּפָּה (wedding canopy).

(See page 59 for a Kabbalat Shabbat playlist.)

Light is a seed,
planted for the
righteous.
one day soon
they will harvest
in joy.

The earth felt joy
The stars sang out
The whole world shouted:
Explode!
Make music!
Sing to God!

My beloved,
spread over me
your shelter of peace.
Be quick, my lover, for
the time has come!

Sing a new song
for all the world's
wonders!
Unite the earth
through sweet sounds
and fair judgments.

(as the sun sets)

Come, my friend, toward the
bride
Let's greet Shabbat!
our spirits bound together —
Come in, bride. Come in!

SOUNDS OF SHABBAT

Lecha Dodi

לְכָה דוֹדִי (Come, My Friend)

Come, my friend, to greet the bride/
Together we will welcome Shabbat

*An Ethiopian Jewish version
of this traditional
Friday-night prayer*

Blessing the Children

As Shabbat begins, many parents give blessings not just over something (like candles, wine, or challah) but to someone. They bless their children. This ritual highlights the sense of touch: Parents place their hands on a child's head or hug the child while giving a blessing.

Some use a traditional text – the oldest Jewish blessing, spoken in ritual settings and homes for more than 3,000 years.

Others improvise, whispering to their children what they appreciate about them and wish for them, what they noticed this week and hope for in the coming week.

This intimate moment is part of a never-ending chain. Our parents and grandparents (and ancestors before them) blessed us with their actions and qualities, and we carry these blessings forward.

The traditional blessing begins with these words:

יְשִׂמְךָ אֱלֹהִים כְּאֶפְרַיִם וְכִמְנַשֶּׁה
יְשִׂמֵךְ אֱלֹהִים כְּשָׂרָה רִבְקָה רָחֵל וְלֵאָה

Yesimcha Elohim ke'Ephraim v'che'Menashe
Yesimech Elohim ke'Sarah, Rivka, Rachel, ve'Leah

May God make you like Ephraim and Menashe*
May God make you like Sarah, Rebecca, Rachel, and Leah**

Here's an alternative version:

May you be like ...

(Choose a person whose qualities will inspire your child.)

It continues with three Hebrew phrases built like a "pyramid": the first phrase with three words, the next with five words, the last with seven words.

יְבָרֶכְךָ יְיָ וְיִשְׁמְרֶךָ
יָאֵר יְיָ פָּנָיו אֵלֶיךָ וִיחֻנֶּךָּ
יִשָּׂא יְיָ פָּנָיו אֵלֶיךָ וְיָשֵׂם לְךָ שָׁלוֹם

Yevarechecha Adonai veyishmerecha
Ya'er Adonai panav eilecha viyechuneka
Yisa Adonai panav eilecha veyasem lecha shalom

May God bless you and keep you
May God shine light on you and be gracious to you
May God turn toward you and grant you peace

You can use this alternative 3-5-7 blessing:

Always be safe
Shine light in the world
And feel truly at peace with yourself

Or give your own blessing:

Here are some prompts:

This week I was proud of you for ...
I hope you'll ...
You are ...

*This line (traditionally said when blessing boys) appears in the Torah when Jacob, at the end of his life, blesses his grandsons Ephraim and Menashe, saying, "By you shall all of Israel give blessings."

**This line (traditionally said when blessing girls) honors the four biblical matriarchs.

A Song for Welcoming Shabbat

Here's a simple way to welcome in Shabbat that most kids will love. Learn this song. (It has three words.)

SOUNDS OF SHABBAT

Shabbat Shalom

שַׁבָּת שָׁלוֹם (Sabbath Peace)

שַׁבָּת שָׁלוֹם – הֵיי!

Shabbat shalom — hey!

Hold your child in your arms during the song. Each time you come to the word hey, toss your child into the air!

Special Shabbat Guests: Angels and a Queen

When everyone gathers at the Shabbat table on Friday night, it's a special moment. For many families, that's a time to take another cue from the Jewish mystics of the Israeli town of Tzfat and welcome special guests into the house: angels.

Jewish angels? The Hebrew Bible is actually quite full of them, each of them defined by a single mission they carry out in the world (for example, telling 90-year-old Sarah that she'll soon bear a child or wrestling with Jacob on the eve of his meeting with his brother Esau).

The angels we invoke at the start of Shabbat also have a single mission: to bring peace into our home. You can also think of angels as our special energies or potential. What did we do with those energies this past week? What will we do with them this coming week?

The song sung to welcome the angels is "Shalom Aleichem" שָׁלוֹם עֲלֵיכֶם ("Peace Be Upon You"). There are many different melodies — you can even learn a family-friendly finger-tapping version! (See page 59 for the Shalom Aleichem Mix playlist.)

Shalom Aleichem

שָׁלוֹם עֲלֵיכֶם מַלְאֲכֵי הַשָּׁרֵת מַלְאֲכֵי עֶלְיוֹן
מִמֶּלֶךְ מַלְכֵי הַמְּלָכִים הַקָּדוֹשׁ בָּרוּךְ הוּא

Shalom aleichem, mal'achei hasharet, mal'achei elyon
Mimelech malchei hamelachim, haKadosh Baruch Hu

Peace be upon you, messengers from above,
angels of the Most High, the Holy One
Come in peace ...
Bless me [and my family] in peace ...
Go in peace ...

(For all four stanzas, see page 7 of the Shabbat Table Companion.)

Who are the angels in your life? (Are any sitting at the Shabbat table with you?)

In the Jewish imagination, another guest shows up as well, bringing majesty and delight in her wake: a queen. (Like the Jewish mystics' Shabbat bride, the queen might represent the feminine aspect of God.) In the Talmud, the core collection of rabbinic writings, we read, "On Sabbath eve, Rabbi Chanina would wrap himself in a special robe and say, 'Let's go out and greet the Sabbath queen.'"

How do you imagine the Shabbat queen? How does she make you feel?

Haim Nahman Bialik, a towering figure of modern Hebrew poetry, wrote this in 1903:

הַחַמָּה מֵרֹאשׁ הָאִילָנוֹת נִסְתַּלְּקָה
בֹּאוּ וְנֵצֵא לִקְרַאת שַׁבָּת הַמַּלְכָּה
הִנֵּה הִיא יוֹרֶדֶת הַקְּדוֹשָׁה, הַבְּרוּכָה
וְעִמָּהּ מַלְאָכִים צְבָא שָׁלוֹם וּמְנוּחָה

Hahama meirosh ha'ilanot nistalka
Bo'u v'neitzei likrat shabbat hamalka
Hinei hi yoredet, hakedosha, habrucha
Ve'ima mal'achim tzva shalom u'menucha

As the sun sinks behind the treetops
Let's go out and greet the Sabbath queen
Descending in holiness and blessing
Surrounded by angels of peace and rest

SOUNDS OF SHABBAT

Shabbat Hamalka

שַׁבָּת הַמַּלְכָּה
(Sabbath Queen)

Bialik's poem set to music

Kiddush קִדּוּשׁ

(Blessing Over Wine or Grape Juice)

The blessing over wine — or *kiddush* קִדּוּשׁ (sanctification) — is the central ritual act of Shabbat. It's traditional to say a blessing over wine to begin Shabbat on Friday night, again in the middle of Shabbat after the morning service, and finally to conclude Shabbat on Saturday night in the *havdalah* הַבְדָּלָה (separation) ceremony.

For millennia Jews have made moments holy or special with wine or grape juice. Since wine "gladdens the human heart" (to quote a biblical psalm), it became the go-to drink for Jewish celebration. At the Shabbat table in a ritual that highlights our sense of taste, we raise our cup and recall that in the creation story God blessed the seventh day. Now, through wine or grape juice, we do as well.

Tips on the blessing over wine or grape juice

THE CUP: While any cup or glass will do, many families have a special cup they use for kiddush — often a silver cup passed down in the family, received as a wedding present, or specially purchased.

FILL IT UP: It's customary to fill the kiddush cup to the brim. This symbolizes the fullness of our lives, a sign of *shefa* (abundance). Some parents place this cup on a small plate and even fill the cup a little beyond the rim (made possible by the laws of surface tension), a real crowd-pleaser with children.

BLESSING: While a father recites kiddush in many families, anyone can do it — or everyone around the table can say it together. It can be done standing or sitting. The blesser raises the kiddush cup while making the blessing. If the cup is totally full, don't worry if it spills a bit onto the plate.

DRINKING: After the blessing, everyone enjoys a sip of wine or grape juice, either from their separate cups or from the kiddush cup. (It's customary to pass the kiddush cup around so everyone can enjoy a sip from that cup or, alternatively, can pour a bit from the kiddush cup into their own cup.) There's even a custom, upon finishing the blessing, for the blesser holding the kiddush cup to drink at least half of its contents in one sip (called *rov kos* רוֹב כּוֹס, "most of the cup") — again, to signify the *shefa* in our lives.

Here is the short blessing over wine or grape juice:

בָּרוּךְ אַתָּה יְיָ אֱלֹהֵינוּ מֶלֶךְ הָעוֹלָם בּוֹרֵא פְּרִי הַגָּפֶן.

Baruch ata Adonai, Eloheinu melech ha'olam, borei p'ri hagafen.

Dear God, Creator of our world, thank You for the delicious fruit that grows on vines.

(For the full version of kiddush, see page 2 of the Shabbat Table Companion.)

The full version of kiddush calls out two main reasons for celebrating Shabbat:

- **The first** is *zikaron lema'aseh vereishit* זִכָּרוֹן לְמַעֲשֵׂה בְרֵאשִׁית – remembering the act of creation, the beauty and awesomeness of the world. This is the Creation motif of kiddush.
- **The second** is *zeicher liyetzi'at mitzrayim* זֵכֶר לִיצִיאַת מִצְרָיִם – remembering the Exodus from Egypt. Because we're aware that once we were enslaved, we extend the right to rest to <u>everyone</u>. That's the Exodus motif of kiddush.

After the work of creation was completed, the seventh day complained, "Master of the Universe, everything you've created comes in couples. Even the days of the week — Sunday with Monday, Tuesday with Wednesday, Thursday with Friday. Only I am left alone!" God replied, "The Jewish people will be your mate."

THE TEN COMMANDMENTS: TAKE TWO

Most people know that the Ten Commandments appear in the Torah (the first five books of the Bible). But did you know that there are two versions of the Ten Commandments?

This is the source of the dual motifs in kiddush. In the Book of Exodus, Moses receives the Ten Commandments at Mount Sinai, and in that version the fourth commandment highlights the theme of Creation. In the Book of Deuteronomy, Moses addresses the nation as he approaches the end of his life and recalls the experience of receiving the Ten Commandments. In that version, the fourth commandment is phrased differently to highlight the Exodus from Egypt.

THE FOURTH COMMANDMENT

(Exodus, chapter 20)

זָכוֹר אֶת יוֹם הַשַּׁבָּת לְקַדְּשׁוֹ *Zachor et yom haShabbat lekadsho*
Remember the Sabbath and make it special. Six days you will work, and the seventh day is God's resting day.

On that day you will refrain from working — you, your children, your workers, your animals, and any visitors to your community.

For God made the heavens, the earth, the sea, and everything in them in six days and then rested on the seventh. And that's why God blessed the Sabbath day and made it holy.

THE FOURTH COMMANDMENT

(Deuteronomy, chapter 5)

שָׁמוֹר אֶת יוֹם הַשַּׁבָּת לְקַדְּשׁוֹ *Shamor et yom haShabbat lekadsho*
Keep the Sabbath and make it special. Six days you will work, and the seventh day is God's resting day.

On that day you will refrain from working — you, your children, your workers, your animals, and any visitors to your community.

Everyone gets to rest so that you might remember what it was like being slaves in Egypt, when God freed you with a mighty hand and an outstretched arm. And that's why God has instructed you to celebrate the Sabbath day.

What do you think it means to "remember Shabbat" and "keep Shabbat"?

Note that one version says "Remember (*zachor* זָכוֹר) the Sabbath" and the other "Keep (*shamor* שָׁמוֹר) the Sabbath." Why these two variations? The Hasidic commentator Sfat Emet says, "We remember the Sabbath all six days of the week, and on the seventh day we get to keep it."

How have you experienced these Shabbat motifs of Creation and Exodus? What "beauty of creation" have you seen? What are ways you rest as a free person?

Washing Hands and Eating Challah

We often ask our kids to wash their hands before eating. On Shabbat, many families turn this act into ritual, celebrating the life-giving power of water and connecting it to another life-sustaining act — a first bite of bread. This ritual also recalls a practice in the ancient Temple in Jerusalem, when priests washed their hands of impurity before handling sacred food and objects.

The handwashing ritual goes like this:

Fill a cup with water, then have each person take turns pouring water from the cup onto their hands (a couple times for each hand). Have each person recite this blessing:

בָּרוּךְ אַתָּה יְיָ אֱלֹהֵינוּ מֶלֶךְ הָעוֹלָם אֲשֶׁר קִדְּשָׁנוּ
בְּמִצְוֹתָיו וְצִוָּנוּ עַל נְטִילַת יָדָיִם.

Baruch ata Adonai, Eloheinu melech ha'olam, asher kideshanu bemitzvotav vetzivanu al netilat yadayim.

Dear God, Creator of our world, thank You for giving us rules that make our lives special and for guiding us in washing hands.

Each person fills the cup for the next person and, after drying their hands on a hand towel, returns to their seat.

By tradition, there's no talking between saying the blessing over handwashing and saying the collective blessing over bread. The reason is that the two blessings — over handwashing and over bread — are one continuous act and should not be interrupted by conversation. That said, during this interval humming is permitted and even encouraged.

(See page 59 for a Wordless Melody [Niggunim] playlist.)

The blessing over bread is a Shabbat favorite in many families. Why? First, the bread is beautiful — a specially braided loaf called challah חַלָּה. The braids hold different meanings for different people. The intertwined strands look like a family in a loving embrace. They can represent the diverse strands of humanity and of the Jewish people. The three overlapping braids can also symbolize three core Jewish values : truth (*emet* אֱמֶת), peace (*shalom* שָׁלוֹם), and justice (*tzedek* צֶדֶק).

If the challah has just been warmed, of course, the smell is wonderful, and the loaf is soft to the touch. Finally, challah is everyone's favorite because it's just plain delicious. So this is a ritual that highlights many senses: sight, smell, touch, and taste.

Here are some rules and customs associated with challah:

DOUBLE THE FUN. In traditional Jewish practice, there's not one but two loaves of challah at the Shabbat table. One reason is to symbolize the two biblical versions of the Fourth Commandment (see pages 40-41): "Remember (*zachor* זָכוֹר) the Sabbath" (Exodus, chapter 20) and "Keep (*shamor* שָׁמוֹר) the Sabbath" (Deuteronomy, chapter 5). Another is a further biblical reference: the double portion of manna that Israelites collected each Friday of their desert wanderings (see page 48). Perhaps most significantly, two loaves help us celebrate abundance — *shefa* — and envision a world in which all will have enough to eat. Whatever the reason, there's no such thing as too much challah. If you have two loaves, raise them so they're touching each other while you say the blessing over bread. (In some families and communities, there's a custom for each person to touch the arm of the person next to them, forming a human chain that extends all the way to the person who's raising the challah and leading the blessing!)

SEPARATION. When baking challah, there's an ancient practice of pinching off a small piece of dough (to be wrapped up or burned) before the braiding begins. This act, *hafrashat challah* הַפְרָשַׁת חַלָּה (separating the challah), recalls the giving of a portion of every loaf to the priests who administered rites at the portable sanctuary in the desert or the Holy Temple in Jerusalem. In Jewish tradition, the moment of pinching off dough is one that holds spiritual power — a time to say a personal prayer for oneself or one's family. If you buy your challah at a Jewish bakery, you should know that the dough may well have been separated in the process of baking your beautiful loaf.

KEEP IT COVERED. It's customary to cover the loaf (or two loaves) of challah with a napkin or a decorated cloth (see page 19). This is a way of beautifying the Shabbat table and, according to Jewish legend, to keep the challah shielded so it doesn't feel slighted by all the attention we've just been paying to the wine. At PJ Library, we like to think of it as a kid-friendly "big reveal": Someone at the table dramatically pulls the cloth off the challah — ta da! — before saying the blessing over bread.

PASS AROUND OR TOSS? After saying the blessing over bread, it's customary to slice the bread and pass around a plate so everyone can take a slice and enjoy their first bite of bread. In some Jewish homes, the custom is different (and slightly outrageous): The blesser tears the challah into pieces and tosses a piece to each person seated at the table. This is a custom that, over time, steadily improves a family's catching skills. (While kids will definitely go for this custom, we'll leave it to parents to decide if they're a pass-around family or a toss family.)

SALT. It's customary to dip challah slices in salt before passing them around. This custom recalls the adding of salt to ritual offerings at the Holy Temple in Jerusalem. When the Temple was destroyed by the Romans in 70 CE, the ancient rabbis reimagined the Shabbat table as the "new altar," and it became customary to put salt on challah. According to the Jewish mystics, it's important to dip challah into salt as opposed to sprinkling salt over the challah. While bread (*lechem* לֶחֶם) and salt (*melach* מֶלַח) are connected — even comprised of the same Hebrew letters rearranged — salt represents law (*din* דִּין) and challah represents kindness (*chesed* חֶסֶד). The challah stays physically higher than the salt because we wish — especially on Shabbat — for the sweetness of challah to overpower the severity of salt. (At the start of a new Jewish year, it's customary to dip challah in honey instead of salt as a sweet beginning to the year.)

Another reason for two loaves of challah (and two candles)

The ritual of blessing the bread (called *hamotzi* הַמּוֹצִיא , Hebrew for "bringing forth") goes like this:

Uncover the challah and raise it high. Recite the blessing:

בָּרוּךְ אַתָּה יְיָ אֱלֹהֵינוּ מֶלֶךְ הָעוֹלָם הַמּוֹצִיא לֶחֶם מִן הָאָרֶץ.

Baruch ata Adonai, Eloheinu melech ha'olam, hamotzi lechem min ha'aretz.

Dear God, Creator of our world, thank You for bringing bread out of the earth.

Now make sure everyone gets enough challah. (And don't forget that challah goes great with butter, hummus, and other dips.)

Why is "breaking bread" together so special?

THE DOUBLE PORTION OF MANNA (EXODUS, CHAPTER 16)

While Shabbat first appears in the creation story in Genesis, the following story in Exodus describes the Jewish people's first experience of Shabbat. (It's also the biblical source for why some families place two loaves of challah on their Shabbat table.) The Jews had been slaves in Egypt for centuries, and this story takes place soon after they crossed the Red Sea to freedom and began their 40-year desert wanderings.

The people went out in the morning and found something covering the ground.

"What's this?" they asked.

Moses replied, "This is the bread (manna) which God has rained down from heaven for you to eat in the wilderness. Gather as much of it as you need to satisfy your hunger."

So each morning they'd rise and gather as much manna as they needed. But on the sixth day, as God instructed, they gathered a **double portion**.

Moses explained, "Tomorrow is the day of rest, a holy Sabbath. On the sixth day, you'll collect two days' worth of food so that on the seventh day you can stay in your place and simply rest."

According to a *midrash* (rabbinic interpretation), manna tasted however each person imagined it to taste.

What would you want your manna to taste like?

The Shabbat Meal Around the World

After the blessing over bread, it's time for Shabbat dinner! We asked PJ Library kids from different countries what their favorite Shabbat foods are, and this is how they responded:

Koby from Brazil
"Coxinhas (teardrop-shaped fried dough stuffed with chicken) – and for dessert, mom's secret cake"

Blake from the UK
"Chopped liver spread on challah with pickled cucumbers"

Alex from Ukraine
"Apple pie with apples soaked in cinnamon"

Amelia from Canada
"My mom's broccoli kugel"

Eyal from Israel
"My dad's chraime (spicy Moroccan fish dish) with lots of garlic"

Ava from Australia
"Chocolate-coated strawberries"

For more Shabbat recipes, visit **pjlibrary.org/shabbat**.

What's your favorite Shabbat food?

After dinner, we thank the cooks for preparing a delicious meal, and it's traditional to sing or say *Birkat Hamazon* בִּרְכַּת הַמָּזוֹן, the Jewish thank-you blessing after a meal. (For an abridged blessing after the meal, see pages 3 and 4 of the Shabbat Table Companion.)

The Traditional Rhythm of Shabbat

The beginning of Shabbat on Friday evening is like a huge sigh of relief. We made it to Shabbat! We can welcome in Shabbat with blessings, songs, and festive food. Some families host guests or go to synagogue for "Welcoming Shabbat" services.

Shabbat morning comes, and different families have different practices. Some go to synagogue, where they hear the reading of the weekly Torah portion. (The Torah is divided into 54 portions, and one — on occasion, two — is read sequentially each Shabbat.) Some have a lazy morning together — what a *mechaya* (Yiddish for "lifesaver")!

The midday meal is known as the "second meal" of Shabbat. It's traditional to recite kiddush over wine or grape juice (see page 5 of the Shabbat Table Companion) and say the blessing over challah bread. The feeling is even more relaxed than Friday night since we're "in the zone," with Shabbat *menucha* stretching both behind us and ahead of us. Some families sing together and say a blessing after the meal.

Even if Saturday morning or afternoon brings work- and chore-related distractions, parents may still manage to find Shabbat day downtime for themselves — to read or be with friends or take a nap by their kids' side (if they're young).

It's customary on Shabbat afternoon to do a little Jewish learning. For centuries, a favorite across both Ashkenazi and Sephardi communities has been the text called *Pirkei Avot* (Ethics of the Ancestors) because it features bite-size Jewish wisdom and requires no background to study. (See Talking Cards on pages 71-72.)

The final meal of Shabbat — called the "third meal" (in Hebrew, *se'udah shlishit* סְעוּדָה שְׁלִישִׁית) — is a light one, and the mood has shifted. We can feel Shabbat slipping away. There's no kiddush recited at this meal, and if songs are sung, they are slower with more of a sense of longing. (See page 59 for a Third Meal Mix playlist.)

On Saturday night, when three stars appear in the sky, Shabbat ends. We say goodbye to Shabbat with a beautiful multisensory ceremony (see page 66) called *havdalah* (separation). We're comforted by the thought that Shabbat will be back again soon.

Presence

פָּנִים

(*panim*, pronounced pah-NEEM)

The third pillar of Shabbat is simply being present — being face-to-face. (The Hebrew word *panim* means "face.")

For families, this can mean simply enjoying each other's presence: hanging out, tuning in, talking about important things that may have gotten lost in the shuffle of the week.

Panim — face — comes from a root meaning "inside." (When you look at a person's face, it often reveals what's inside.) Traditionally when we're together at the Shabbat table, we take time to reveal a bit of what's inside us. We can ask each other, "What was something new or special or challenging that happened this week?" We can wonder about something in this week's Torah portion; all opinions are welcome since it is said that the Torah has "70 faces." Or we can set words aside and try something we'd seldom do during the week — pick a melody and sing together.

There's an old tradition to invite people we want to get to know better — in Hebrew, *panim hadashot* פָּנִים חֲדָשׁוֹת or "new faces" — for a Shabbat meal. In a modern twist on *panim*, we have a new tradition to video chat before Shabbat with grandparents or other relatives and close friends who live far away.

> No system that engages a variety of human beings can be absolutely perfect. But Shabbat comes close ... It is a day of release and re-energizing, of family and community, of spiritual and physical well-being ... Without it I could not live.
>
> — Blu Greenberg (contemporary author and feminist activist)

SOUNDS OF SHABBAT

Hinei Ma Tov

הִנֵּה מַה טּוֹב

How good and pleasant it is/
For families to come together

A popular Hebrew folk song based on a phrase from a biblical psalm

How does your family like to come together on Shabbat?

Panim points us toward the **connection** we want to make on Shabbat — the intimacy we can feel together and the moments of self-care we can give ourselves.

The Hasidic commentator Sfat Emet says that just as Shabbat celebrates the completion of heaven and earth, so does it call out to us to seek our own completion. In his view, it is on Shabbat that the "power of our higher self" comes down and connects with our everyday self, deepening our relationships and our self-awareness.

Shabbat is a weekly invitation to families to be together in ways that matter to them. To let their hair down. To talk. To play. To make music. To ask important questions. To let each other be heard. To tell stories. To see beautiful things. To check in. To think about the world together.

Shabbat is an ideal time for "active listening," not to jump to how you'll reply to your child but simply and fully to listen to them. The quality of attention you give them — your Shabbat *panim* — will help your child better articulate thoughts and feelings.

In this section of the guide, Presence, you'll find some tips on connecting as a family on Shabbat.

But first we turn to the biblical book of the Song of Songs, which is read every Shabbat all over the world in Sephardi and Mizrahi communities. The Song of Songs is a beautiful poem about two lovers. The Jewish sages viewed it as a metaphor for the love between God and the Jewish people. At PJ Library, we reimagine this traditional Shabbat text as expressive of the love between parents and children.

The Song of Songs

I was asleep but my heart was awake.
Listen! My beloved knocks.

My beloved is like a gazelle or a young deer
Leaping over mountains, bounding over hills.
You capture my heart with one glance of your eyes.

Let us go to the garden
To see if the vine has flowered
And the pomegranates are in bloom.

Like an apple tree among the trees of the forest,
I delight to sit in your shade.

SOUNDS OF SHABBAT

Bo'i Legani

בּוֹאִי לְגַנִּי

(Come to My Garden)

A traditional Mizrahi piyyut *(sung poem)*

Let me see your face.
Your voice is sweet, your face is beautiful.
Your eyes are doves, your legs are pillars,
your hair is like a flock of goats.

Tell me, whom I love so well:
Where do you pasture your sheep?
Where do you rest them at noon?

Your left hand was under my head.
Your right arm embraced me.
I held you fast, I would not let you go.

No flood can sweep away my love.
No river can drown it.

I am my beloved's, and my beloved is mine.
אֲנִי לְדוֹדִי וְדוֹדִי לִי
Ani ledodi vedodi li

(See page 59 for a Song of Songs Mix playlist.)

13 Ways for Families to Connect on Shabbat

1 Eat good food. (Desserts taste especially yummy on Shabbat.)

2 Take a family nap.

3 Take a great walk. Perhaps explore some beautiful place in nature.

4 Read out loud together. (Did someone say "PJ Library"?)

5 Have interesting conversations (see page 58).

6 Turn off phones and screens to give each other our full attention.

7 Take on a project. For example, assemble a puzzle. Visit an elderly neighbor. Do some volunteering.

8 Take time to pray (at a synagogue or home) **or do something quiet and reflective** like family yoga or meditation.

9 Get together with nice people.

10 Tell stories (see page 60).

11 Sing (see page 59).

12 Play games (see page 62).

13 Do something you love together.

Shabbat Conversation

Let's talk! Here are prompts for family or one-on-one conversations, around the Shabbat table or anytime on Shabbat. Pick one question and let everyone share their response. (You can download these prompts at **pjlibrary.org/shabbat.**)

What was something good (even wonderful!) that happened this week? What was something that was hard or challenging for you, and how did you handle it?

What special person did you spend time with this week? What did you do together?

What were you most proud of this week?

What amazed you this week? What amused you this week?

Did you meet anyone new this week? Who did you enjoy saying hello to?

What do you need a break from this Shabbat?

What question did you ask this week? What new thought did you have? What's something new you learned?

What is something kind you did for someone this week? What's something kind that someone did for you this week?

A VISUALIZATION

(For older kids — this is challenging for adults too!)
Close your eyes and go back over the week in your mind. What's something that happened on Sunday? (Give people a moment to think about each day.) On Monday? On Tuesday? On Wednesday? On Thursday? On Friday? Now hold all those thoughts — and let them all go. It's Shabbat.

Talking Cards

There are more conversations waiting for you on pages 71-72. Check them out!

Shabbat Songs

One of the best ways to add Shabbat joy (*oneg*) is through music. Some families like to hit PLAY on a Shabbat playlist; others take out instruments and jam. The most traditional way to make music on Shabbat is simply to sing.

> Get into the habit of singing a tune. It will give you new life and fill you with joy. Even if you can't sing well, sing!
>
> — Rabbi Nachman of Breslav
> (18th-century Hasidic master)

PJ Library has customized playlists to enhance your Shabbat experience. Find them all in one easy place.

- **Sounds of Shabbat**
- **Shabbat Table Companion — Blessings, Traditional Songs, More Songs**
- **Shabbat Spirit**
- **Friday Night Favorites**
- ***Kabbalat Shabbat* (Welcoming Shabbat)**
- ***Shalom Aleichem* Mix**
- **Wordless Melodies (*Niggunim*)**
- **Song of Songs Mix**
- **Top Tunes: Summer Camp**
- **Top Tunes: Sephardi-Mizrahi**
- **Third Meal Mix**
- ***Havdalah* (Shabbat Conclusion)**

Shabbat Stories

Here are some Shabbat-themed stories to tell on Shabbat — when you're not busy reading your favorite PJ Library books!

The Cow Who Wouldn't Work on Shabbat

Shlomit the farmer loved her milky-white cow Halvi. Every Shabbat when Shlomit rested from her farm work, Halvi rested too. They were real Shabbat buddies!

But one year when it rained so little that Shlomit's crops didn't grow well, Shlomit found herself running out of money. She had no choice but to sell Halvi to her neighbor Yoni. Yoni did not care about Shabbat, and he woke early Shabbat morning to bring Halvi with him to work in the fields. Halvi didn't move. Yoni pulled and pulled and pulled, but Halvi wouldn't budge.

Yoni came running to Shlomit. "The cow you sold me is lazy!" he said in frustration. "No, she's not," replied Shlomit. "She works hard all week long, but when Shabbat comes, she rests."

Yoni was very moved by this. He started calling Halvi his Shabbat cow, and over time, Yoni decided that he, too, would rest on Shabbat.

(Adapted from a story in the Talmud, the core book of rabbinic wisdom)

What's something you've learned from an animal?

The Shaky Shabbat Table

Ora always set a beautiful Shabbat table with glowing candles, freshly picked flowers, wine, challah, and delicious food. She loved having guests. This particular Shabbat, Ora had a crowd of friends at her table, and she also invited a young man from her community who had never been to a Shabbat meal.

When it came time to say kiddush, the blessing over the wine, the young man lifted his glass along with everyone else, but it slipped out of his hand. Red wine spilled onto Ora's beautiful white tablecloth.

Seeing the young man's embarrassment, Ora gently nudged the table leg, slightly rocking her kiddush cup, which was full to the brim with wine. A little more red wine "accidentally" spilled onto the tablecloth. The young man looked relieved. Ora laughed. "Oh my! The table must be a little shaky tonight."

Then Ora sang kiddush. And everyone had a wonderful meal, especially the young man.

(Adapted from a 19th-century Polish anecdote)

When have you felt embarrassed? Has anyone ever helped spare you embarrassment?

A Shabbat Dilemma (What Would You Do?)

Maury and Robbie were on a long trek in the mountains, far away from everything. For many days they had no phone reception, and they lost track of which day it was. It was their practice on Shabbat to take a day off from hiking, but they suddenly realized, "When is Shabbat?" They didn't know anymore.

Maury said, "Let's count six days, and then take a day to rest. That's what God did. After creating the world in six days, God rested for a day."

Robbie said, "No, let's take a day of rest now, and then count six days until the next one. That's what Adam and Eve did. They were created on the sixth day, just before the first Shabbat began, and after Shabbat they counted the days until the next Shabbat."

Maury and Robbie needed to make a decision — wait six days and then keep Shabbat, or keep Shabbat now.

(Adapted from a story in the Talmud)

If you were Maury and Robbie, what would you do, and why?

The Magic River

After Rome conquered the land of Israel, the Roman governor Turnus Rufus brought Rabbi Akiva before him on Shabbat. He asked Rabbi Akiva, "What makes the day you call Shabbat different from other days?" Rabbi Akiva — who always liked to answer a question with a question — said, "Governor, what makes you more important than other people?" Turnus Rufus answered, "I am more important because my master, the emperor of Rome, wants it that way." Rabbi Akiva added, "And Shabbat is different than all other days because my master, the Master of the Universe, wants it that way."

Turnus Rufus continued, "But who is to say that today is Shabbat? Perhaps it falls on a different day of the week — like Tuesday or Wednesday." Rabbi Akiva replied, "We know because of a river called Sambatyon. All week long the currents of this river rush with enormous force, pushing giant rocks around. But when the sun sets on Friday night, the river grows completely calm."

The Jewish legend of the Sambatyon River is ancient, retold in the Talmud as in the version above and by generations of Jewish scholars and mystics, including the great medieval Spanish commentator Nachmanides. The historian Flavius Josephus describes the Sambatyon in reverse — a river that is still all week and flows only on Shabbat!

What else besides a river could you imagine resting on Shabbat?

Stories from the Torah

The Torah (the first five books of the Bible) is the story of the Jewish people — from Abraham and Sarah's journey to Canaan until the end of the Jewish people's 40 years of wandering — and it's traditional to read another section of that story each Shabbat.

It's special to explore Torah stories together on Shabbat. If your family is interested in picture books based on Torah stories and other online Torah-related resources, visit **pjlibrary.org/shabbat**.

Shabbat Search-and-Find

In this picture, there are 25 hidden Shabbat items. Can you find them all?

- 1 setting sun
- 1 tzedakah box
- 1 welcome mat
- Flowers
- 1 nice shirt
- 1 pair of Shabbat candlesticks
- 2 angels
- 1 crown (Shabbat queen's)
- 1 wedding veil (Shabbat bride's)
- 1 pair of hands
- 1 kiddush cup
- 1 prayer shawl (tallit)
- 2 loaves of challah
- 1 musical note
- 1 Torah scroll
- 3 PJ Library books
- 3 stars
- 1 havdalah candle
- 1 spice box

To download a PDF of this list (with check boxes), visit **pjlibrary.org/shabbat**.

SHABBAT SHALOM
PJ

Broadening the Circle: Shabbat in Community

The Jewish people goes by many names, such as the "people of Israel" (*am Yisrael* עַם יִשְׂרָאֵל) or the "people of the book" (*am hasefer* עַם הַסֵּפֶר). Another name is *mekadshei shvi'i* מְקַדְּשֵׁי שְׁבִיעִי — the ones who sanctify the seventh day.

For many families, the face-to-face nature of Shabbat extends beyond the home and includes being connected to community. This connection might be with a local synagogue, which offers activities for families with young children such as Tot Shabbat, family or children's prayer services and learning, and other family programs. Or this connection might be with a set of friends for occasional Shabbat get-togethers or even regular Shabbat gatherings.

What do families do when they get together on Shabbat? It depends on the families. Some just share a Shabbat meal. Others do a mix of activities: praying, singing, storytelling, having discussions, playing games, hiking. As your family grows, you can experiment and change the kind of get-togethers you have.

[At a Shabbat dinner] community is convened in a single evening. Since the Shabbat dinner community has no fixed membership rules, anyone can join and feel like a member in good standing. It engenders great pride in Jewish tradition and culture, while stretching the very meaning of Jewishness in marvelous ways.

— Rabbi Steve Greenberg (contemporary teacher and author)

What Shabbat activities would you want to share with other families?

For Parents

Vulnerability and Intimacy on Shabbat

by Rabbi Steve Cohen

Love and intimacy are the great blessings of being human, but they're not always simple. To protect ourselves from hurt, we build up walls that separate us: from strangers, naturally, but also from our friends and family. If we hope for loving connection, we need to make ourselves vulnerable. Shabbat is an occasion for both vulnerability and intimacy. In the unprogrammed, unrushed minutes and hours of Shabbat, we may suddenly find ourselves face-to-face with the people we love.

When my wife and I were first married, we found the Friday-night ritual challenging. It felt awkward, like we were pretending. That moment of self-consciousness was a time of great vulnerability. Then we had kids, and they taught us the holiness of play. At 2 and 3 years old, children take play seriously; our kids recognized Shabbat rituals as sacred play. Eventually, from them, we learned to stop worrying and have fun with the rituals. We learned to combine playfulness with reverence.

When our kids were a bit older, we formed a Shabbat-morning gathering for prayer, singing, discussion, and food. In the afternoon, the group would gather in a park or at one of our homes to eat, talk, and hang out. Sometimes, I would fall asleep — not squirreled away in a bedroom but on the grass or in a chair, surrounded by friends and children, vulnerable yet safe enough to let down my guard. In this Shabbat bubble, I could close my eyes and drift off.

The kids kept growing (as they do). After our eldest child left for college, our second was still at home. It was not a time of deep communication between him and us. There was a lot of silence, and we worried whether we would ever be relaxed with each other again. We did insist that he be home for Shabbat dinner every week, even if he was going out with friends afterward. Once at the Shabbat table, I asked him, "Can you tell us something about your inner life?" He smiled and began to share with us some of his big questions. For that to happen, I had to risk that he would reject my question, and he had to risk opening himself up to our opinions.

Shabbat can offer opportunities for openness, vulnerability, and intimacy. You might be exhausted or distracted or unready to let your guard down. It will take a small act of courage to look each other in the eyes or share what you are really thinking and feeling. But that is the act of courage required to connect to another soul, and Shabbat can give you the time and space to make that act of courage possible.

Rabbi Steve Cohen has served as rabbi at Congregation B'nai B'rith in Santa Barbara, California, and Santa Barbara Hillel.

Havdalah

הַבְדָּלָה

Havdalah (pronounced hahv-dah-LAH)
Separation, or Concluding Shabbat

When three stars appear in the sky on Saturday night, Shabbat is over. In that moment, we distinguish between the time we call Shabbat שַׁבָּת and that which we consider "everyday time" (*yemei hol* יְמֵי חוֹל).

We make a separation between the two, treasuring the pleasures we experienced on Shabbat and — recharged and revitalized — looking forward to a new week and all it will bring.

The short ceremony that marks this transition is a favorite among many families (and certainly among Jewish camps). Why?

1. It's very easy to do, taking only a few minutes.
2. It's beautifully multisensory, with a captivating light to gaze at, fragrant spices to smell, and sweet grape juice to drink. Each ritual item has its own simple symbolism.
3. It offers a lovely way for families to share a meaningful Jewish moment, savor a last bit of Shabbat joy, and enter a new week with feelings of love, hope, and togetherness.

The ceremony is done sitting or standing around a table. At Jewish camps, the ceremony is usually performed while standing in a big circle — which can feel like one giant group hug — and culminates in havdalah songs and dancing.

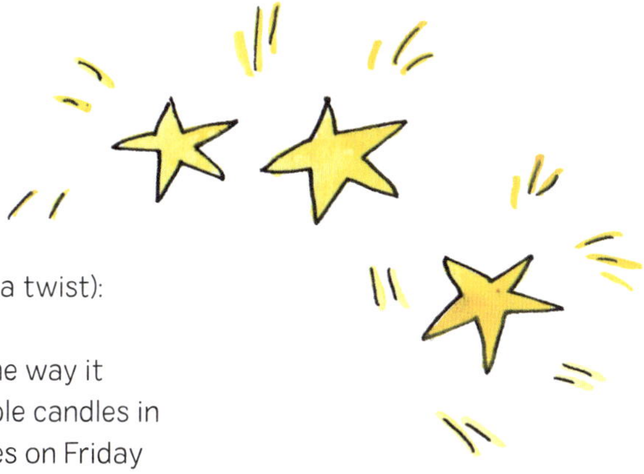

The three ritual elements of havdalah may feel familiar (with a twist):

CANDLELIGHT is the way Shabbat began, so now it's also the way it ends — the glowing bookends of Shabbat. Instead of two simple candles in candlesticks — what we usually light when blessing the candles on Friday night — we now hold one long candle that is braided (like a challah!) and has many wicks. The multiple wicks represent how distinct souls come together to celebrate Shabbat. In a family, we're each unique, yet we're all "in it together" — and likewise for the Jewish people and for humanity. The intense multiwick light casts dancing shadows on the walls and, during the ceremony, on the fingers of our outstretched hands. This contrast between light and shadow represents how each week we separate between the work week and the day of rest, a true differentiation of time.

WINE OR GRAPE JUICE is the go-to Jewish drink to sanctify any special moment. We drink wine or grape juice at kiddush on Friday night (and for some families, on Shabbat day as well). At havdalah, instead of simply drinking the grape juice, we also douse the candle's flame in it, a sizzling marker of the end of Shabbat and the beginning of a fresh new week.

AROMATIC SPICES let us recall the wonderful smells of Shabbat cooking and challah baking. At havdalah, when we gather spices (often cloves and cinnamon) in a spice box or pass around freshly picked spices from our garden, we're inviting the sweet fragrance and simple joys of Shabbat to linger as we enter a new week. And remember the classic idea of receiving a "second soul" on Shabbat? An additional explanation for spices at havdalah is to revive us — sort of like smelling salts, but sweeter — as we feel that second soul departing from us.

To perform the havdalah ceremony, you'll need the following:

- **A CUP OF GRAPE JUICE OR WINE.** (Use a kiddush cup or any cup.)
- **A MULTIWICK HAVDALAH CANDLE** with a plate or piece of tinfoil to drip onto. (You can buy or make the special braided havdalah candle. If you don't have one, simply light two regular candles and hold their wicks together, creating a multiwick effect.)
- **PLEASANT-SMELLING SPICES** placed in a traditional spice box or any other container. (For a simple DIY spice sachet, see the accompanying activity at right.) You can also just pass around aromatic strands and leaves from your garden — sage, rosemary, lemongrass ... anything goes!

Make a Spice Sachet for Havdalah

Cut a 10-inch square of cheesecloth, tulle, or fabric. Place a couple of tablespoons of sweet spices (cinnamon, cloves, nutmeg) in the middle, then gather the edges and twist them together to close the sachet. Secure the sachet with a rubber band, then tie a short length of ribbon around it.

The Havdalah Ceremony

This is a basic havdalah ceremony. For fuller blessings and songs, see page 6 of the Shabbat Table Companion.

To begin, light the candle and lower or turn off the lights. Let candlelight fill the room and illuminate faces.

Raise the cup of grape juice or wine and say or sing,

בָּרוּךְ אַתָּה יְיָ אֱלֹהֵינוּ מֶלֶךְ הָעוֹלָם בּוֹרֵא פְּרִי הַגָּפֶן.

Baruch ata Adonai, Eloheinu melech ha'olam, borei p'ri hagafen.

Dear God, Creator of our world, thank You for the delicious fruit that grows on vines.

Don't drink — yet. Raise the spices and say or sing,

בָּרוּךְ אַתָּה יְיָ אֱלֹהֵינוּ מֶלֶךְ הָעוֹלָם בּוֹרֵא מִינֵי בְשָׂמִים.

Baruch ata Adonai, Eloheinu melech ha'olam, borei minei vesamim.

Dear God, Creator of our world, thank You for the amazing smell of these spices.

Pass the spices around so everyone can take a deep sniff. (Carry the scent of Shabbat with you into the new week.)

Raise the multiwick candle. Everyone should hold their hands in front of them, palms up, and curl their fingers slightly, watching shadows form on their palms. (Light contrasts with shadow, just as Shabbat contrasts with the rest of the week.)

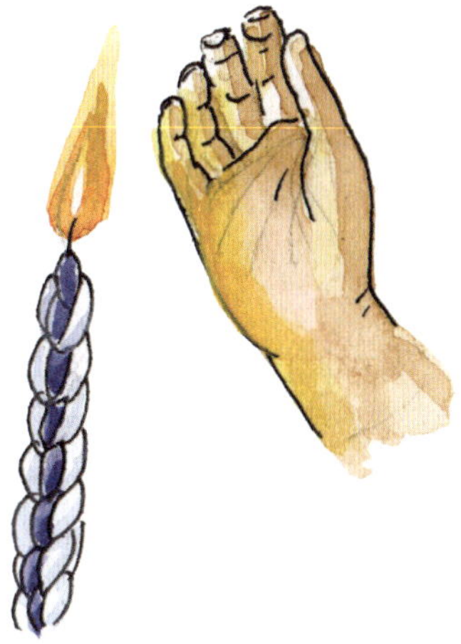

Say or sing,

בָּרוּךְ אַתָּה יְיָ אֱלֹהֵינוּ מֶלֶךְ הָעוֹלָם בּוֹרֵא מְאוֹרֵי הָאֵשׁ.

Baruch ata Adonai, Eloheinu melech ha'olam, borei me'orei ha'eish.

Dear God, Creator of our world, thank You for the beauty of these fiery lights.

Now raise the cup again and say or sing,

בָּרוּךְ אַתָּה יְיָ אֱלֹהֵינוּ מֶלֶךְ הָעוֹלָם הַמַּבְדִּיל בֵּין קֹדֶשׁ לְחֹל.

Baruch ata Adonai, Eloheinu melech ha'olam, hamavdil bein kodesh lehol.

Dear God, Creator of our world, thank You for separating the holy from the everyday.

Take a tiny sip of grape juice or wine, making sure to leave a bit in the cup.

Dip the candle into the wine or grape juice, dousing the flame. Or pour that remaining wine or juice onto the plate for dousing the flame.

Everyone says, *"Shavua tov"* (shah-VOO-ah TOHV) שָׁבוּעַ טוֹב — have a good week!

It's traditional to finish havdalah by singing in the new week. One popular havdalah song is about Elijah the Prophet, the same mysterious figure who visits our Passover seder each year and represents Jewish dreams for a future filled with peace and justice. (For lyrics, see page 6 of the Shabbat Table Companion.)

Hands on a New Week: A Family Game

It can also be fun to conclude havdalah with a quick game of Knots. Everyone stands in a circle, stretches their hands toward the middle, and finds two different hands to hold onto (though it can't be a hand of the person standing next to you). Without letting go of any hands, the group needs to "unknot" itself, so in the end everyone is holding onto the hands of the person next to them. (Spoiler alert: This may require some twisting around and even stepping over outstretched hands.) When the perfectly unknotted circle is formed, a new week can begin!

Epilogue

Closer to Home

In the Jewish imagination, Shabbat is an epic idea:

- In the Genesis narrative, God creates the world in six days and rests on the seventh. But Jewish medieval poets added that God thought up the idea of Shabbat even before starting to create the world. In other words, the idea of Shabbat sets the entire universe in motion.

- At the other end of the timeline, our prophets and ancient rabbis imagined a better future — a deeply longed-for World to Come — that looked a lot like Shabbat, a time of peace and harmony, rippling with delight.

- In the Torah, the holiest day of the Jewish year (Yom Kippur, the Day of Atonement) is called *Shabbat Shabbaton* שַׁבַּת שַׁבָּתוֹן, "the Sabbath of Sabbaths." Like Shabbat, it's a time for letting go and rising above. On Shabbat we let go of the pressures of the week; on Yom Kippur we let go of grudges and bad habits accumulated over the course of a year.

- The Torah mandates a "Shabbat for the earth" (in Hebrew, *shmita* שְׁמִטָּה): every seventh year, we're commanded to give the land a yearlong rest.

In these and other ways, Shabbat has fueled Jewish visions of personal, environmental, and social change.

But for most families with young children, Shabbat is about things closer to home: how the whole house feels different when Shabbat candles are lit, how our kids' faces light up (like Shabbat candles!) when they take a bite of warm challah, how sweet it feels to say to someone — especially to our kids — "Shabbat shalom!"

Returning each week to familiar Shabbat rituals, whether it's blessing our children or reading a favorite storybook together, can be deeply comforting. Yet the regularity of Shabbat poses an opportunity and a gentle challenge as well: Why not try something new this Shabbat? We can try making the dish we loved eating at our friend's house or introduce ourselves to that new family in the neighborhood or at synagogue. We can read a Torah story we've never explored together or step outside on Saturday evening to see who can spot the first three stars to appear.

There are so many simple ways — old and new — to find rest (*menucha* מְנוּחָה), count our blessings (*shefa* שֶׁפַע), and enjoy quality time together (*panim* פָּנִים). In doing these, we can help instill in our kids active joy, quiet gratitude, and both openness and rootedness.

In much of Jewish literature, Shabbat is called *Shabbat kodesh* שַׁבַּת קֹדֶשׁ, the holy Sabbath. Many of us might feel that we don't really understand what *holy* means. But then again, when we're cuddling on the couch with our child after a delicious Shabbat meal ... maybe we actually do.